Alone Together

Aaron Ruth

alone

you dont love me anymore

if i look closely enough
i can still see your fingerprints
stained on my skin
like i am just an exhibit
that was placed in
the wrong museum
and you were curious enough
to touch
but never curious enough
to feel

i used to hate my reflection
until i saw myself
holding your hand in it

since you went away
i make sure
to walk by every mirror i see
slowly

it is the only time
i can see you again

but deep down i know
it is for this same reason
that your house is full
of broken mirrors

i never thought i could miss
what i never had
but ever since you left
i cannot stop reminiscing
about the memories
of our future

you pulled my strings
and made these fragile bones
dance for you
despite the fact that there
was never any music

but that did not stop your hands
from getting too intimate
with my identity

i should not have allowed myself
to become so defenseless
but the moment you so slyly
took control of my life
i was trapped
in our graceful tragedy

i do not remember my name
but you tell me
that i am lovely

so i kept dancing
and only stopped when you became
tired of manipulating me

but without your hands
guiding my every movement
i am so out of place
trying to dance
in a world with no music

i used to stutter on flower petals
a garden flowing in my lungs

you placed butterflies in my heart
back when we were young

you used to be the sunlight
that i needed to bloom

now dead roses wilt inside my veins
my skeleton my tomb

i am still trying to make sense
of this mess you left me to clean up

as my hands bloody
from picking up the shards
of our memories
i cannot help but laugh
at the irony of all this

i was always willing
to clean up after your mistakes
regardless of how deeply
they cut into me

these wounds hurt like hell
but i will still put myself
through anything
to try to keep us together

emptiness cuts deeper than glass

the loneliness
will absolutely destroy you
it will grab ahold of your heart
and cast it out into the darkness
the voices in your head
will grow arms
and their hands
will smother your lungs
until breathing
is but a memory

you will feel abandonment
like smoke that has no choice
but to leave the candle
it has grown to love
when the fire is put out

you will have no choice
you will be powerless
you will want answers
but you will not be able to choose
which questions to ask

this loneliness is like no other

and perhaps worst of all
the last thought you will have
before the darkness
finally collapses on you
will be of her
and how when she left
she took the light with her

once you left
i thought i could
find solace in gardens
until i saw your face
in every flower

each a reminder that sometimes
it is better
to leave the flower to be beautiful
and alone
than to pick it up
and have it be beautiful
and lonely

both you
and the flower
made me realize
that even if i love something
with all my heart

it will forget how to breathe
if it abandons its roots

perhaps the hardest part
of all this

is realizing
that he is able to give you
what i never could

i said i had no favorite color
as we walked that afternoon
you stopped me mid-sentence
how can that be true?

you see blue is my favorite color
and certainly the most appealing
for it is the only color
that also is a feeling

but those days are long gone
and you have left without goodbye
yet still your voice haunts me
when i look towards the sky

no matter how many times
i try to escape this hue
it is all because of you
i only feel but blue

how is it
that i am the poet
yet he is the one
that always seems
to say the right words

i put so much effort
into making the heart on my sleeve
seem fashionable to you
that when i finally
stripped down for you
there was nothing left
for you to get intimate with

exposed

maybe all this time
i was living a façade
and i am not as brave
as i had once thought i was

maybe i cannot do this alone

i cannot do this alone

they say
that when you see a star
it is already dead
and even though it is beautiful
it is nonexistent

the first time
you told me you loved me
my stomach
lost its sense of gravity
and an endless galaxy
was created in my bones

but little did i know
that when you see a star
it is already dead
and even though it is beautiful
it is nonexistent

in a somber room
illuminated by a hint of moonlight
i try my best to remember
just how you looked
when you were still
between these sheets
with me

a shadowed silhouette
illuminated by a hint of moonlight
you tasted like forgiveness
and reminded this body
what it felt like
to hold something so fragile
yet so powerfully beautiful

my favorite mosaic
if you would only come back
i will remind you that
in times in which you feel broken
i am broken too
but our fragments fit together
like the angels planned
for this jigsaw puzzle love
to find a way

i promise
if you would only come back

a descending leaf burnt red
another victim of autumns exhale

a sinking leaf burnt red
no voice in how the future unfolds

a collapsing leaf burnt red
succumbs as biting winds prevail

a fallen leaf burnt red
incarcerated by the earths firm hold

as winter flaunts her beauty
in the crisp night sky above

a burnt red leaf
bares a shattered heart

desperately gazing upward
towards its futile frigid love

hidden in cold sheets
i fictionalize this moment
by pretending you are still here
to kiss my skin before the sun can

but empty fantasies
welcome haunting realities
in which i only feel lifeless lips

a kiss
from the memory
of what once was

time slips off her clothes
she will help make you forget
what you felt with *her*

haiku #1

you have made me realize
how weak i am
by begging me
to give all my strength
to burdens
that were too heavy
to ever lift

if lies could cry
i think the ocean
would help convince me
that what we had is still real

you whisper sweet fiction
until i drown
in the only thing that is not there
but somehow
i can still feel

i cannot believe
the truth about this
but deep down i know

i hold on to the last of us
with all my strength
because i am far too weak
to let you go

a dream
painted by sand between toes
and the color of you

i fall asleep to remember
palm trees above
and footprints below

hands held like sand dollars
in the palms of little ones

a dream
as true as midsummer moonlight
but as fleeting
as the sapphire waves

dandelion eyes
gone without a trace

trust it was for the better
that i blew you away

as the asphalt beneath your feet
begins to crumble
and you collapse into
whatever lies below

i hope you reach
for dimly lit memories of us
that you once held so closely
as you fall into
the epilogue of this life

i pray
in your new beginnings
you will remember me
as being much better than i was

remember me as the one
that always caught you
when you fell

even though
i was more of a silhouette
than a parachute to you

here
but never really here

maybe upon death
we will come back to earth
as the opposite of what
we are now

i will return
as a puppet
with no strings attached

and you will return
as my puppeteer
hopelessly chasing control

but you
as i have learned in this life
will never catch me

and after awhile
you will come to realize
how weary i grew
from pointlessly chasing after you

your eyes hold me at gunpoint
yell
give me all your love or ill shoot

i spend every night
trying to cover
all of my bullet holes
with band aids and confidence

i promise
i am trying my best
to give you everything i am

to show you
that you are the only person
i would die for

even if that means
i have to be the one
that continues to provide you
the ammunition

everything was black
everything was grey
i was told from early age
nothing gold can stay

but then

i looked over my shoulder
and lo and behold
the black and grey were replaced
with vivid colors of untold

you looked like a promise
your eyes a lovely shade
green whispering with blue
with every blink i fell for jade

her lips made me fall weak
desire like that of a starlet
a colorful passion took my breath
with every kiss i fell for scarlet

under innocent white linen
you loved with no restrain
intoxicated by ivory skin
with every night i fell for champagne

your joy became my own
we laughed as dusk stole light of day
for the first time in my life
certainly something gold would stay

then

one cloudy afternoon
a kiss a rushed goodbye
you left me alone and abandoned
under a daunting charcoal sky

raindrops showered my skin
hurriedly i ran for cover
for with each invading drop
i lost a hint of your color

i reached no safe haven
no solace could be found
i was forcefully cleansed of you
as i collapsed upon the ground

when finally i awoke
the rain had passed on through
frantically i searched my skin
but found no shade of you

everything is black
everything is grey
the rainbow came before the rain
nothing gold can stay

we departed
as quickly as we emerged
yet i still feel your name
circulating in my bloodstream

recently
i have been holding my breath

i tell myself
if i can hold it long enough
maybe i will pass out

if i am lucky
i will develop amnesia

at this point
that seems to be
the only cure for you

lose-lose situation

tell me everything i want to hear
say it quietly
let me sip slowly
and delight in these exquisite lies

i hate the taste of deceit
but i indulge nevertheless

empty yourself to me
then act as everyone else has
and leave me alone

alone

defenseless against the
double edged sword
that is regret

is fear real
or is it not

is fear
merely the absence of courage
or is fear
its own entity

because lately
i can feel it

strong
breathing down my neck
while the taste
of courageous blood
still lingers
fresh in its jaws

you know how i get when im alone

when it is two in the morning
and you
are tossing and turning in bed
you can tell yourself
it is insomnia

you can tell yourself
it is just the demons and angels
playing tug of war with your mind

you can tell yourself
whatever you need to hear

but we both know
that when it is two in the morning
and you cannot fall asleep

you will end up thinking about how
my chest
was always your favorite pillow

my heartbeat
your favorite lullaby

and you will realize
that you made a mistake
when you decided
to put our love to rest

i am afraid of all this
of me
of you
this world
the future

what if i fail
what if i fall
what if you get tired of me

because everything
is always ending
and things are always dying
and if i am honest
i struggle sometimes
to see the point
in all of this

i still feel you around me

i see your shadow
everywhere i look
and i cannot help but think
that i
have done all these things before
with you by my side

because every new memory i make
contains a remnant of you

déjà vu

the loneliest feeling in the world

feeling trapped
within yourself

no vacancy / no exit

how free it would feel
to wear skin you have not touched
but burn scars dont fade

haiku #2

eventually
the tragedy of love will strike

and we will have no choice
but to fly away
from the one
who showed us our wings

once upon a midnight
when the time felt opportune
i beckoned towards the sky
in hopes of talking with the moon

for weeks I had been trying
but yet to no avail
as i dropped my head in defeat
i heard a woeful wail

i called out to the crescent
as i marveled at his glory
and much to my surprise
he told me a somber story

centuries ago when i was youthful
before i ascended high
i wished upon the stars
that i could live up in the sky

but do not be deceived
for it was only for one purpose
i so loved the shining sun
i deeply craved to kiss her surface

day in and day out
she shined fiercely yet so tender
and when she vanished every night
i dreamt only of her splendor

40

i prayed and prayed for change
that i could become her companion
to live eternally by her side
my life on earth i would abandon

my prayers were soon answered
suddenly we were face to face
and she softly scarred my skin
as we met in warm embrace

i offered her my hand
and asked her to be my lover
but her answer split me in two
i am in love with another

in shame i ran away
in the darkness i would hide
yet even away from her presence
i saw her when i closed my eyes

since then i have been a slave
to the desolate midnight sky
and while each night i shine for all
i am vastly empty inside

the moon finished his tale
and silently wept about his fate
but was utterly surprised
when i told him i can relate

for i had also loved a light
and like you for her love i pled
only to be coldly told
she had loved another instead

moon we are so distant
yet we are one in the same
we both bear a blue heart
but must shine despite the pain

often
i feel like a penny on the street

thousands of people walking by
but no one taking the time
to pick me up

just because my heads down

shattered broken gone
but my lips curve as i lie
and say i am fine

haiku #3

how dare you
set a fire in my soul
and ignite
every inch of my bones
with the sole intention
of walking away

how dare you
abandon me
when it was you
that set my timid heart ablaze

i am sitting in this fireproof room
alone
while these third degree burns
blister my skin

i have never felt more cold

you cannot teach a heart
to love abandon

but still
i miss you so much

stockholm syndrome

you used to crawl with me
and often we would try
but we could never fly

we grew close
we were afraid
so you went off to hide

you reemerged
butterfly
i looked up and saw you in the sky

but deep down
i still hold on
to when we were younger

i still cant fly
but you
made me think i could

am i selfish
if i say i wish we could go back
to the past

they say that insanity
is doing the same thing
over and over again
in hopes of obtaining new results

so i cant blame them
when they call me irresponsible
and reckless
and stupid

for repeatedly running back
to the prison
from which i have been set free

they tell me that i am naive
for returning to these chains

but they dont know you
like i do

like a cherry blossom
in early spring
a delicate touch
full of history

you appeared with beauty
painted on your lips
and i yearned to discover
the taste of fragility

but with a kiss
that whispered solace
you vanished as quickly
as you had come

Alone

I have spent years
trying to convince myself
to fall in love with my insecurities

I have spent years
trying to convince my brain
that sometimes
it is okay to let the heart win

And while I'm not perfect
I am finally starting to realize
that my reflection is but a flower

It will change with seasons

Some days
it will be withered
but on other days
it will bloom

And while I pray
for more days of blooming

I must remember
that even in seasons of wilting

I am alive

There is beauty
in the unpredictable
and fascination in the faith
that leads me to reach
higher and higher

And while I have yet to discover
what exactly it is
I am searching for

Something tells me that one day
I will not find it
but instead
it will find me
and it will answer all my questions
and be everything I will ever need

Be Patient

Today
I decide
to finally take my own advice
and I challenge myself to live
as I have never lived before

Today
is the beginning
of something incredible

I am on the path to greatness
and cannot be stopped

I understand
that I still have a long way to go
but as I look ahead
to the finish line

I realize
that the most important step I took
was the first

To End, You Must Begin

All this noise is only a distraction
from the things that matter most

That is why
when you are comfortably
alone
with the world at your feet
the sound of silence is deafening

Do not make a sound

Feel the symphony of silence
surrounding you

These times matter most

The blood
running through your veins
is not there to remind you
of yesterday

You are today

Stop looking back
and be here

The loudest people
have the least to say

Chase silence—
for there is an abundance of life
when voices are dead

Growing up as a boy
means being told
that true masculinity
is choosing a woman
that will simply tell me
exactly what I want to hear
and blissfully admire my strengths

But I have discovered
it is far more important
to find someone that will
empower my vulnerabilities
push the limits of my comfort zone
expand my creativity
and encourage me to grow
as I do the same for her

1 Corinthians 11:11

So often
we are imprisoned
hearts incarcerated by expectation

How frightening it is
to think of what we could become
if we took the chains off our hearts
and started to live freely

We hope to leave behind
a river of overflowing memories
when we depart

Yet we live so timidly
almost as if we believe
we will be here forever

Take no notice
of what the world tells you to be—
it is irrelevant

Be something
they have never seen before

Be something
they cannot handle

Whether or not
you think your story
is unique

It is

Use it to change your world
and eventually
the world

Being lost can be dangerous
until you reach that place
you always knew you were
destined to arrive at

Even if
you did not always quite know
how to get there

Only until I found
my identity in God
was I able to look back
and see how lost
I truly was for all those years

Come As You Are, For He Forgives

What we can control
is how we love

No matter the situation
we can always choose to be
carefree and lighthearted lovers
of this life
and of one another

Love is eternal

It cannot be broken
or infringed upon

Life can be broken
and ruined
in so many disastrous ways

But still
we can choose to love
with every ounce of life
in our bodies

Because at the end of the day
we is all we've got

1 Corinthians 13

A world filled with color
yet we refuse to see in anything
other than black and white

A world filled with music
yet we put the oldies on repeat
expecting to hear a different song

Calculated chaos—
a world transfixed by tradition

A world with
an orchestrated disillusionment
that we can see new lands
without leaving the comfort
of our own shore

I am still trying to figure out
if it is harder
or easier
to wait for something
when I do not know
for how long
I will be waiting

You can watch a flower for days
and think that no progress
is being made towards the bloom

But the flower knows otherwise

There is a place beyond the sunset
where serenity
is found on a warm smile
and love
is as delicate yet as bountiful
as a cool summer's breeze

Where restless bones
find solace in welcoming arms
and although it is unknown why
arriving
feels like coming back home

Ascension / Heaven

Loving you is complicated

You have proven to me
that sometimes
recognition is more fulfilling
than a first impression

On the days in which I come
face to face with a stranger
I reach for the yesterday
in which I stared at familiarity

You are trying your best to learn
how to love
and you are learning
that it is more difficult than it sounds

Yet you continue to learn
and grow
and for that
I admire and thank you

Mirror, Mirror

Softly
ever so softly
I tip-toe on shallow waters
with a solemn curiosity
of what may lie
in the depths below my feet

But onward I walk
step by step
for the light within me
can overcome what is lurking
in the shadows
drooling with hunger
waiting impatiently for me to slip
and descend
into the clutches of the barren void

But let the shadows starve
for they will have to wait
another day
and another
and another

For today
I walk without trembling
I follow the footsteps
of the ones who went before me

I follow the One leading me
to safe havens
and softly
ever so softly
His grace saves me again and again

This morning
I looked into the mirror
and recognized the face
looking back

It made me wonder
how long it has been
since I have seen myself
in the reflection

But that—
the confusion
the misalignment
the disapproval—
is in the past

Today
there is recognition

Today
I am me

It is strictly up to you
and you alone
to make sure
that you are living the life
you have always dreamed of

Please remember that brokenness
does not symbolize
the tragic end of life

Rather
being broken is the first step
of an intensely promising
reawakening of hope

It may take years
of navigating valleys and mountains
but eventually
this adventure will make sense

It may not seem like it now
but clarity is coming
and the view from this place
will be like nothing of which
you have ever seen

Remain Patient

It is all a constant cycle
of trying to remember
that even though
this all will end

That is not a good enough reason
to let it go away
untouched

Destruction is not permanent

I am strong enough
to make mountains
out of the ashes

I am strong enough
to turn broken
into beautiful

Mantra

You know how I get when I'm alone

It is okay
to feel incomplete at times

Breathe—
a new day is approaching

Are you happy?

A yes or no question
but people insist
on making it so much more
complicated
than that

Do Something About It

How can we understand
the magnitude of this moment
if we do not shake hands
with the daunting reality
that this moment
will never happen again?

Sometimes
purpose looks less like
discovering the evasive road
that will lead you
into ultimate success
and more like a slow afternoon
when you realize
you are doing the most you can
with the blessings
you have been given

I am caught in the eye of the storm
calm
but I look around
and see brilliant chaos
everywhere I turn

I will soon be uprooted
and I will not resist these winds
when they come

For this
is what I have been
patiently waiting for

When Love Arrives

The best example
of beautiful destruction
is when two strangers
with untamed hearts
lock eyes for the very first time

And in that moment
they know
they feel
that there is no possible way
their fiery hearts
can be restrained

And in that moment
they silently agree
that the vast world
is theirs to burn

They say
when I fall in love
I will feel butterflies
in my stomach

They say
it is a feeling
full of uneasy excitement
for the future

They say
having the butterflies
is *magical*

They
are lucky

As of now
my butterflies either have
broken wings
or my stomach is home
to eager caterpillars

I hope it is the latter

I am ready for you
whoever you are

I am ready
to feel my stomach flutter

I dream of arms
that are strong enough
to pull me closer
when the word
commitment
slithers into the air

I dream of shoulders
that know how
to not only catch tears
but burdens as well

I dream of lips
that smile unapologetically
when they realize that they
have the power
to turn my flaws
into goosebumps

I dream of lips
that are not afraid
to abuse that power

I dream of eyes
that can paint pictures
of both security and wanderlust
with a simple look

I dream of a heart
that will take the time
to teach mine
how to dance

I dream of a kiss
that can hold my oxygen
for ransom
but has the grace
to return it to me
even in moments
when I do not want it back

I dream of a touch
that can mend skin back together
for the times that my old skeletons
come out to haunt my confidence

I dream of a love
that can turn my dreams
into reality

I dream of a reality
that makes dreaming futile
because everything
I can possibly crave
is already holding my hand

Alone Together

I know it is late
but do you think you could stay
and hold my hand
just a little bit longer?

The Beginning

A glance
A smile
A whisper
A first date
A sweaty palm
A first kiss
A sleepless night
A bed, unmade
A new beginning

Some nights
when you are gone
I stand under the clouds
and pretend the raindrops
running down my skin
are your fingers

I have grown to love
dancing in the rain

Perhaps
remaining still
is not in our blood

But that does not stop me
from fighting the current
every single time
I am forced to leave your side

I let my fingers
run through your hair
as if flipping through the pages
of your past

I look into your eyes
and steal a glimpse of innocence

And while your scars
whisper memories of destruction

Your lips foreshadow stories
of optimism

The Taste of Hope

I turn your face towards mine
and look into your eyes
like they are the last pair
I will ever see

I take your breath away
along with your dress
I was always told
that the prettiest dresses
are worn
to be taken off

We are alone together
and although we are touching
I am still dying to get closer

Then I remember
that you are still there
and I am still here

And yet again
you have seduced me
from across the room

In winter wild
you were warm
a crackling fire
a perfect storm

In summer warm
you were wild
a sandy walk
a heart reconciled

Through each season
you have stayed
a faithful answer
to a prayer prayed

Honestly
it really doesn't matter.
I just need to be next to you…
I need to be by your side.
I can't explain it,
but just being near you is always
exactly what I need,
and it is slowly starting to become
exactly what I want.

Read 1:37 AM

You are visual poetry

You told me you liked sunflowers
because they always face the sun
as if growing towards innocence
is a natural instinct for them

But there are places
where the sun does not reach
and from this place
I took my first steps

Sometimes
I am afraid to face what is right
even though I know it will help me
be better than my yesterday

Afraid
of what will nurture my growth
but despite the fear of goodness
I search for the light

From the shadows I grew
but it was not until I saw you
that my petals raised their hands
reaching for your saving grace

As raindrops danced
like grains of sand
floating mindlessly
in the vast ocean

As teardrops fell
like reminders of divide
flowing purposely down
your rosy cheeks

You whispered that our love
was simply incapable of lasting
and I agreed

But then with a steady finger
I removed the mixture
of teardrops and raindrops
from your face
as if it were the last time
I would ever hold
any part of you

And in that moment
we realized
that we could not go on
without being
by each other's side

And with tired eyes
and restless souls
we declared our leap
into the unknown realms
of incapable love
with a warm kiss
sealed with frigid lips

It's funny
that I put so much effort
into putting on clothes
that I know you'll love
just in hopes
that you will take them
right off

Tell me everything
about your day
every day

I do not want
anything about us
to be a long story short

Even though
by opening myself up for you
I am becoming more susceptible
to the fall

Exposing the deepest parts
of myself
to potentially feel you
under my skin
is well worth the risk

If indeed
love is blind
I will learn Braille
by tracing your thighs
and we can communicate
with our body language
the goosebumps
telling me everything
I need to know

If indeed
love is blind
I will still find you
amongst a crowd
and tell you
that you
are the most beautiful woman
I have ever seen

Body / Language

I am still in disbelief
as to how you convinced me
that my flaws
are something worth embracing
but ever since you made your way
through my walls
the mask I once wore daily
has been collecting dust

How blessed am I
to have someone
that suppresses all my anxiety
every time she speaks

I wish nothing more
than to be a bird
free to roam around

I wish nothing more
than to reach heights so high
I never touch back on ground

I wish nothing more
than to rise and gaze
from a greater point of view

I wish nothing more
than to fly away
and maybe that's what I'll do

I wish nothing more
than to freely soar
as happy as can be

I wish nothing more
but wouldn't want to soar
if you weren't soaring next to me

You know how I get when I'm alone

May I have this dance?
A young daydreamer trembles
I have been practicing for you
I vow to be gentle

In the silence that follows
a disillusionment spreads
for this is not how this played out
in the daydreamer's head

Yet patiently he remained
as he waited for an answer
from the lips of his muse
and wishfully, his dancer

But dreamer, why me?
You must be mistaken!
She looks to his eyes
yet he is unshaken

This mustn't be real
for she cannot believe
someone craving her heart
is an idea she cannot conceive

She sidesteps from mirrors
treats her reflection with cruelty
but little did she know
to him, she is beauty

He offers his hand
and the music fades out
she takes it so gently
as she drowns in self-doubt

They slowly begin to dance
a beautiful pirouette
and what happened then
she will soon not forget

He whispered softly in her ear
suddenly, she felt free
as a midsummer's wind
gliding with ease

She gazed in his eyes
and she saw forever
she felt the rest of her life
as timid lips came together

After all this time
the daydreamer's dream came true
for his love smiled as he whispered
It's always been you

I plan on loving you until…

The Only Poem I've Ever Finished

I will always be in disbelief
as to how she can make lust
appear out of thin air
by whispering to me
across a busy room
without saying a word
but rather
with a look that teases

We are alone here...
What are you going to do about it?

I want to
kiss your flaws
bite the lips of your blemishes
make love to your insecurities
and scratch stories of strength
and desire
into the back of your vulnerabilities
until your skin begins to sing songs
of resurrected courage

I want to give
your weaknesses goosebumps
and I promise
I will not stop
until the seducing power
of passion
makes your heart skip a beat
as you remember what it feels like
to live with self-confidence

Muse

And what was I
but a rogue drop of water
violently leaving the past
to find a new home
wherever that may be

And what were you
but a tender flower
ready to offer love
to anything that would
fall into you and stay awhile
whatever that may be

And what did we have
but a crash landing
in which you showed me
shades of yellow
I had never before seen
as you caressed
my shape-shifting walls

And what is love
but a new life
alone together
with you
when your petals
sing songs of home
and I fall asleep
listening to the gentle lullabies

I believe it was a Wednesday
we built a fort out of pillows
and blankets
just outside of the living room

We crawled inside
and told each other jokes
we have heard
hundreds of times before
but for whatever reason
we could not help but laugh again
as if it were the first time

We sat in there for hours
and as the room grew dim
we used flashlights
to see each other
and I remember thinking
that the shadow puppet show
you put on
was spectacular

I never wanted that night to end

Then it happened

When I messed up a joke
and you fell back onto a pillow
dying of laughter
and you turned to face me
and that was the exact moment
I knew

There are only two things
that can hijack my heart
and crash it into my lungs
forcing words of love
to desperately fill the air
as if looking for a girl like you
to come along
and listen to them

What were the chances
that both of these objects
that have the power
to make my walls
so weak
would end up on your face
staring back at me
with a look that says
I am listening
Please…tell me more

There is nothing
that compares to the feeling I get
every time you call me the nickname
that only we know

Only your lips
can soften my edges

Melting my skin
until I flow like a river

Following the current
of your kiss

Only your voice
can make my skin surrender

And looking back now
I thank God for the Alone
a time to prepare

*Haiku #4 / Realizing I Wasn't Ready
to Love Yet, Despite My Thinking
Otherwise / 2 Timothy 2:22*

They can see us

But all we can see is each other

Alone Together in a Crowded Room

I see my future looking like…

Baking cookies on rainy days

Grey sweater, messy hair—
it matches the bed

I see me
pulling you closer
as we dance in the living room
our hearts in synchronized motion

The living room—
how appropriate

Every palpitation feels purposeful
when you are by my side

A reminder
that I have the opportunity
to grow a day older
with your hand in mine
and that has always been enough for
me

I see you in a white dress
seeing me in a tuxedo
waiting impatiently
for the chance to tell the pastor
I do

I see you
when I look at our daughter—
you'll have the same eyes

Maybe one day
she will realize that is why
I can never look away from her

I see you
gray hair, messy sweater—
it still matches the bed

I guess some things never change

I am trying my hardest
for you

I know sometimes
that simply is not good enough
but I promise I will always try
for you

I hope that
the thought of us being
alone together
is enough to make your legs
untangle like a blank page

Longing for my poetry
to leave its mark

My words will move like hands
and I will recite this poetry
until these metaphors undress you
and you find yourself stranded
in a sea of blankets on my bed

My words will move like lips
and I will recite this poetry
until these promises kiss your skin
making sure to taste
every single spot

Breathe—
try to breathe

I know you
have been waiting for me
for this
just as long as I have

Feel your chest rise
as breaths get harder to hold
and your pulse
matches the rhythm of mine

I will whisper these secrets
in your ear
until you forget about this world

My words are the kiss of a wildfire
spreading over your skin
a poetic inferno
until your body is ablaze
melting my lips
as pleasure burns at the touch

Do not be afraid
to fight fire with fire
and scar my skin
for eternity

The moment
when everything comes together
and I look at you
and I do not just see life
but I can *feel* it
and you speak
and the voice
fills me with harmony

And just when I think
it cannot get any better
I remember that
I am yours
alone
and you are mine
the same
and only we can hear
the symphony we create

There is no one else
I would rather share silence with

There are days
when the skeletons in my closet
come together
and try to convince me
that the past is something
worth giving a second chance

There are days
I want to listen

On the days I cannot remember
where my strength is
I look to you

And somehow
you always know
exactly what to say
to put the haunting mistakes
back in the past
right where they belong

Every time my eyes meet yours
it feels like the first time
and I begin to daydream
about seventy years from now
when we
are telling our grandchildren
stories of our youthful love

As we tell them the tales
and laugh at what we choose
to keep from them—
our little secrets—
I will look through the wrinkles
and see the young girl
that had the audacity
to call my reckless arms home

And I will fall all over again
like it was the first time

I'm so selfish

I can only think of you

You took the time
to give attention
to parts of me
that no one else
ever seemed to notice

Because of that
you have learned my dreams
my fears
my strengths
and my weaknesses

You have shown me
that this is how
humans are supposed to love
wildly and attentively

Because of you
I realize we were created to be

Alone together

Alone Together

Author's Note

I wrote this book to explore the
concepts of "alone" and "lonely"

Throughout the past couple years, I
have experienced the three chapters
in this book: alone, Alone, and Alone
Together

It is important to understand that no
season lasts forever.
Just as important is this: There is
something for you in each season

With that being said, in times of
suffocating loneliness, there is still
someone out there that cares about
you

Do not be a voice unheard
Help is out there

The National Suicide Prevention
Hotline is ready to give you hope

Call 1-800-273-8255 or visit
www.suicidepreventionlifeline.org
if you need hope

Acknowledgments

To God,
none of this is possible without You.
I pray that You speak through these
poems and use my work to change
lives

To my family,
you have shown me exactly what it
means to love. I will always treasure
the memories we share. I like you
and I love you

To my friends,
you have been there through it all.
Thank you for being patient with me
during moments I had to sacrifice
some time. I love you and (usually)
like you

To Justin,
my greatest friend in the creative
world and most talented producer I
know. Thank you for your
inspiration and support. Your drive
and determination is unparalleled.
Support him at
IG: byjayjames
Twitter: byjayjames

To Presli,
thank you for reviewing each line
over and over again. I will always be
here to support you, whatever that
may look like. One day, I hope to
edit the book you write

To Annika,
thank you for the incredible cover
and efforts towards this book. You
perfectly captured the concept of
"alone together." You have a very
bright future ahead of you

To every person that reads this book,
I cannot express my thanks enough.
Your support and encouragement
means the world to me. I can only
hope I can return the favor in some
way

Remember,
you are not alone

About the Author

Aaron Ruth was raised in Murrieta, California by Kurt and Cyndi Ruth

He will soon graduate from San Diego Christian College receiving his Bachelor's Degree in English

He was baptized on March 5, 2017 at The Rock Church in El Cajon, California. On this day, he realized that he would never again be alone, for the weight of the world had been lifted off of his shoulders

Alone Together is Ruth's first book and is roughly five years in the making. He hopes to publish more books in the future, each with a message that can help people in whatever season they may be in. He believes, above all, we must love and care for each other

Colossians 3:14

Twitter
@aaronruth_

Instagram
@aaronruthpoetry

Blog:
aaronruthpoetry.blogspot.com